Anonymous

The Tarot of Paul Christian

Anonymous

The Tarot of Paul Christian

ISBN/EAN: 9783337426934

Printed in Europe, USA, Canada, Australia, Japan

Cover: Foto ©Thomas Meinert / pixelio.de

More available books at **www.hansebooks.com**

The Tarot of Paul Christian

These Major Arcana descriptions are found in *Historie de la Magie, du monde Surnaturel et de la fatalité a travers les Temps et les Peuples.* (*History of Magic, the Supernatural World and Fate, through Times and Peoples*) by Paul Christian (Jean-Baptiste Pitois) -1870.

Illustrations of Tarot Cards by J. Augustus Knapp & Manly P. Hall -1928

ARCANUM I

[Letter *Athoim* (A)--Number 1]

THE MAGUS: *Will*

DIVINE WORLD - The absolute Being who contains and from whom flows the infinity of all possible things.

INTELLECTUAL WORLD - Unity, the principle and synthesis of numbers; the Will, principle of action.

PHYSICAL WORLD - Man, the highest of all living creatures, called upon to raise himself, by a perpetual expansion of his faculties, into the concentric spheres of the Absolute.

Arcanum I is represented by the Magus, the type of the perfect man, in full possession of his physical and moral faculties. He is represented standing upright, in the attitude of will proceeding to action. He wears a white robe, image of purity. His belt is a serpent biting its tail: the symbol of eternity. His forehead is enclosed in a fillet of gold, signifying light; this expresses the continuum in which all created things revolve. The Magus holds in his right hand a golden sceptre, image of command, raised towards the heavens in a gesture of aspiration towards knowledge, wisdom and power; the index finger of the left hand points to the ground, signifying that the mission of the perfect man is to reign over the material world. This double gesture means that human will ought to be the earthly reflection of the divine will, promoting good and preventing evil.

Before the Magus on a cubic stone are placed a goblet, a sword and a shekel--a golden coin in whose center a cross is engraved. The goblet signifies the mixture of passions contributing to happiness or misfortune, according to whether we are their masters or their slaves. The sword symbolizes labor, the striving that overcomes obstacles and the tests that pain makes us undergo. The shekel is the image of aspirations fulfilled, works accomplished, the apex of power attained by perseverance and will-power. The cross, seal of the infinite with which the shekel is engraved, announces the future ascent of that power into the spheres of the future.

Remember, then, son of earth, that man should, like God, act without ceasing. To will nothing and do nothing is more fatal than to will and do ill. If the Magus should appear in the prophetic signs of thy horoscope, it announces that a firm will and faith in yourself, guided by reason and a love of justice will conduct you to the end that you wish to attain and will preserve you from the perils of the way.

ARCANUM II

[Letter *Beinthin* (B)--Number 2]

THE DOOR OF THE OCCULT
SANCTUARY: *Knowledge*

DIVINE WORLD - The consciousness of the absolute Being who embraces the three periods of all manifestations: the past, the present and the future.

INTELLECTUAL WORLD - The Binary, reflection of Unity; Knowledge, perception of visible and invisible things.

PHYSICAL WORLD - Woman, the matrix of Man, who joins herself with him in a similar destiny.

Arcanum II is represented by a woman seated on the threshold of the temple of Isis, between two columns. The column on her right is red: this signifies purity of spirit. The column on her left is black, and represents the night of chaos, the impure spirit's captivity in the bonds of material things. The woman is crowned by a tiara surmounted by a crescent moon covered by a veil whose folds fall over her face. She wears on her breast the solar cross and carries on her knees an open book which she half-covers with her cloak. This symbolic figure personifies occult science waiting for the initiate on the threshold of the sanctuary of Isis to communicate to him nature's secrets. The solar cross signifies the fecundation of matter by spirit; it expresses also, as the seal of the infinite, the fact that knowledge proceeds from God, and is, like its Source, without bounds. The veil enveloping the tiara and falling over the face means that truth hides itself from the sight of profane curiosity. The book half-hidden by the cloak signifies that the mysteries reveal themselves only in solitude to the wise man who wraps himself in the cloak of silent meditation.

Remember, then, son of earth, that the mind is enlightened in seeking God with the eyes of the will. God has said, "Let there be Light," and light inundated space. Man should say, "Let truth show itself and good come to me." And if man possesses a healthy will, he will see the truth shine, and guided by it will attain all to which he aspires.

If Arcanum 2 appears in your horoscope, knock resolutely on the door of the future and it will be opened unto you; but study long and carefully the path you are to tread. Turn your face towards the sun of Justice and the knowledge of what is true shall be given unto you. Speak to no one of your purpose, so that it may not be given over to the contradiction of men.

ARCANUM III

[Letter *Gomor* (G)--Number 3]

ISIS-URANIA: *Action*

DIVINE WORLD - The supreme Power balanced by the eternally active Mind and by absolute Wisdom.

INTELLECTUAL WORLD - The universal fecundity of the supreme Being.

PHYSICAL WORLD - Nature in labor, the germination of the acts that are to spring from the Will.

Arcanum III is represented by a woman seated at the center of a blazing sun; she is crowned by twelve stars and her feet rest on the moon. She is the personification of universal fecundity. The sun is the emblem of creative strength; the crown of stars symbolizes, by the number 12, the houses or stations through which the sun travels year after year. This woman, celestial Isis or Nature, carries a sceptre surmounted by a globe: it is the sign of her perpetual activity over things born and unborn. On her other band she bears an eagle, symbol of the heights to which spirit may soar. The moon beneath her feet signifies the weakness of matter and its domination by the Spirit.

Remember, son of Earth, that to affirm what is true and to desire what is just is half-way towards creating those things; to deny them is to condemn oneself to destruction. If Arcanum III manifests itself among the signs of your horoscope, you may hope for success in your enterprises, provided that you know how to unite productive activity with the rectitude of spirit that makes your labors bear fruit.

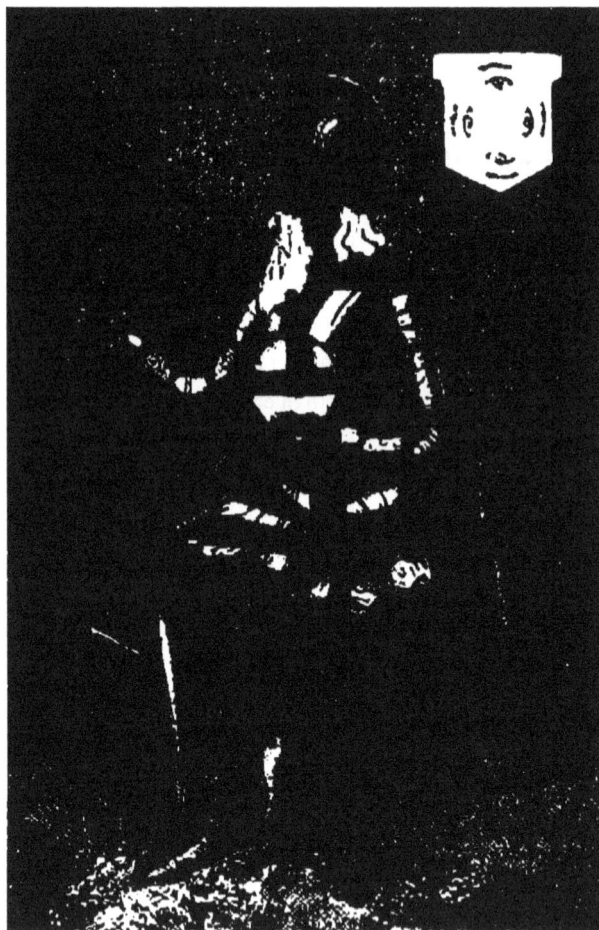

ARCANUM IV

[Letter *Dinain* (D)--Number 4]

THE CUBIC STONE: *Realisation*

DIVINE WORLD - The perpetual and hierarchical realization of the virtues contained in the absolute Being.

INTELLECTUAL WORLD - The realization of the ideas of the contingent Being by the quadruple effort of the spirit: Affirmation, Negation, Discussion, Solution.

PHYSICAL WORLD - The realization of the actions directed by the knowledge of Truth, the love of Justice, the strength of the Will and the work of the Organs.

Arcanum IV is represented by a man wearing a helmet surmounted by a crown. He is seated on a cubical stone. His right hand holds a sceptre and his right leg is bent and rests on the other in the form of a cross. The cubical stone, image of the perfect solid, signifies the accomplishment of human labors. The crowned helmet is the emblem of the strength that conquers power. This dominating figure holds the sceptre of Isis, and the stone which serves him as a throne signifies conquered matter. The cross described by the position of his limbs symbolizes the four elements and the expansion of human power in every direction.

Remember, Son of Earth, that nothing can resist a firm will, which has as its support the knowledge of the true and the just. The struggle to realize these things is more than a right, it is a duty. The man who triumphs in this struggle does no more than accomplish his mission here on earth; he who succumbs in his devotion to the cause acquires immortality. If Arcanum IV appears in your horoscope, it signifies that the realization of your hopes depends on a being more powerful than yourself: seek and find him, and he will be your support.

ARCANUM V

[Letter *Eni* (E)--Number 5]

THE MASTER OF THE ARCANA:
Occult Inspiration

DIVINE WORLD - The universal Law, regulating the infinite manifestations of the Being in the unity of substance.

INTELLECTUAL WORLD - Religion, the relationship of the Absolute to the relative Being, the Infinite to the Finite.

PHYSICAL WORLD - Inspiration; the test of man by liberty of action in the closed circle of the universal law.

Arcanum V is represented by the image of the Hierophant (Master of the Sacred Mysteries). This prince of occult doctrine is seated between the two columns of the sanctuary. He is leaning on a cross with three horizontals and describes with the index finger of his right hand the sign of silence on his breast. At his feet two men have prostrated themselves, one clothed in red, the other in black. The Hierophant represents the Genius of good intentions and the spirit of conscience; his gesture invites to meditation, to listen to the voice of the heavens in the silence of the passions and of the instincts of the flesh. The column on his right symbolizes the divine law; the one on the left signifies freedom to obey or disobey. The triple cross is the emblem of God pervading the three worlds in order to produce in them all the manifestations of life. The two men, one red, the other black, represent the genii of Light and of Darkness, both of whom obey the Master of the Arcana.

Remember, son of Earth, that before saying a man is happy or unhappy you must know to what use he puts his will, for all men create their lives in the image of their works. The genius of Good is on your right, Evil on your left: their voices can only be heard by your conscience. Meditate, and it will tell you what they say.

ARCANUM VI

[Letter *Ur* (U, V)--Number 6]

THE Two ROADS: *The Ordeal*

DIVINE WORLD - The knowledge of Good and Evil.

INTELLECTUAL WORLD - The balance of Necessity and Liberty.

PHYSICAL WORLD - The antagonism of natural forces, the chain of cause and effect.

Arcanum VI is represented by a man standing motionless at a crossroads. His eyes are fixed upon the earth, his arms crossed on his breast. Two women, one on his right, one on his left, stand each with a hand on his shoulder, pointing out to him one of the two roads. The woman on his right has a fillet of gold around her forehead: she personifies virtue. The one on the left is crowned with vine-leaves and represents the temptations of vice. Above and behind this group the genius of Justice, borne on a nimbus of blazing light, is drawing his bow and directs the arrow of punishment at Vice. The whole scene expresses the struggle between the passions and conscience.

Remember, son of Earth, that for the ordinary man vice has a greater attraction than virtue. If Arcanum VI appears in your horoscope, take care to keep your resolutions. Obstacles bar the road to happiness; contrary influences hover around you; your will vacillates between opposing sides. In all things indecision is more fatal than the wrong choice. Advance or retreat, but never hesitate; remember that a chain of flowers is more difficult to break than a chain of iron.

ARCANUM VII

[Letter *Zain* (Z)--Number 7]

THE CHARIOT OF OSIRIS: *Victory*

DIVINE WORLD - The Septenary, the domination of Spirit over Nature.

INTELLECTUAL WORLD - The Priesthood and the Empire.

PHYSICAL WORLD - The submission of the elements and the forces of matter to the Intelligence and to the labors of Man.

Arcanum VII is represented by a war-chariot, square in shape, surmounted by a starred baldaquin upheld by four columns. In this chariot an armed conqueror advances carrying a sceptre and a sword in his hands. He is crowned with a fillet of gold ornamented at five points by three pentagrams or golden stars. The square chariot symbolizes the work accomplished by the will which has overcome all obstacles. The four columns supporting the starry canopy represent the four elements conquered by the Master of the sceptre and the sword. On the square representing the front of the chariot is drawn a sphere upheld by two outstretched wings, sign of the limitless exaltation of human power in the infinity of space and time. The crown of gold on the conqueror's head signifies the possession of intellectual illumination which gives light to all the arcana of Chance. The three stars which decorate it at five points symbolize Power balanced by Mind and Wisdom. Three squares are engraved on the breast-plate: they signify rectitude of Judgment, Will and Action which gives the Power of which the breast-plate is the emblem. The lifted sword is the sign of victory. The sceptre, crowned by a triangle, symbol of the Spirit, by a square, symbol of Matter, and by a circle, symbol of Eternity, signifies the perpetual domination of the Mind over the forces of Nature. Two sphinxes, one white, the other black, are harnessed to the chariot. The former symbolizes Good, the latter Evil--the one conquered, the other vanquished--both having become the servants of the Magus who has triumphed over his ordeals.

Remember, son of the Earth, that the empire of the world belongs to those who possess a sovereign Mind, that is to say, the light which illuminates the mysteries of life. By overcoming your obstacles you will overthrow your enemies, and all your wishes shall be realized, if you go towards the future with courage reinforced by the consciousness of doing right.

ARCANUM VIII

[Letter *Heletha* (H)--Number 8]

THEMIS: *Equilibrium*

DIVINE WORLD - Absolute Justice

INTELLECTUAL WORLD - Attraction and Repulsion.

PHYSICAL WORLD - The relative, fallible and narrow Justice which is man's.

Arcanum VIII is represented by a woman seated on a throne wearing a crown armed with spear-points: she holds in her right hand an upward-pointing sword and in the left a pair of scales. It is the ancient symbol of Justice weighing in the balance the deeds of men, and as a counter-weight opposing evil with the sword of expiation. Justice, which proceeds from God, is the stabilizing reaction which restores order, equilibrium between right and duty. The sword is here a sign of protection for the righteous and of warning for the sinful. The eyes of Justice are covered with a bandage to show that she weighs and strikes without taking into account the conventional differences established by men.

Remember, son of Earth, that to be victorious and to overcome your obstacles is only a part of the human task. If you would wish to accomplish it entirely, you must establish a balance between the forces you set in motion. Every action produces its reaction, and the Will must foresee the onslaught of contrary forces in time to lessen or check it. All future things hang in the balance between Good and Evil. The Mind that cannot find equilibrium resembles a sun in eclipse.

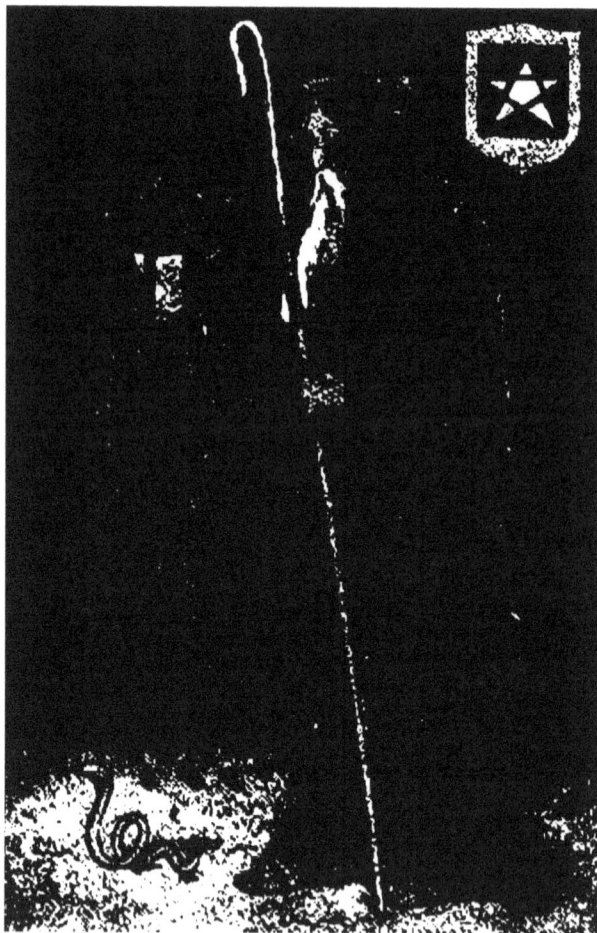

ARCANUM IX

[Letter *Thela* (TH)--Number 9]

THE VEILED LAMP: *Prudence*

DIVINE WORLD - Absolute Wisdom.

INTELLECTUAL WORLD - Prudence, the governor of the Will.

PHYSICAL WORLD - Circumspection, guide to Action.

Arcanum IX is represented by an old man who walks leaning on a stick and holding in front of him a lighted lantern half-hidden by his cloak. This old man personifies experience acquired in the labors of life. The lighted lantern signifies the light of the mind which should illuminate the past, the present and the future. The cloak that half conceals it signifies discretion. The stick symbolizes the support given by prudence to the man who does not reveal his purpose.

Remember, son of Earth, that Prudence is the armor of the Wise. Circumspection allows him to avoid reefs or pitfalls and to be forewarned of treachery. Take it for your guide in all your actions, even in the smallest things. Nothing lacks importance: a pebble may overturn the chariot in which the master of the world is riding. Remember that if Speech is silver, Silence is golden.

ARCANUM X

[Letter *Ioithi* (I. J. Y)--Number 10]

THE SPHINX: *Fortune*

DIVINE WORLD - The active principle that animates all beings.

INTELLECTUAL WORLD - Ruling Authority.

PHYSICAL WORLD - Good or evil Fortune.

Arcanum X is represented by a wheel suspended by its axle between two columns. On the right Hermanubis, the Spirit of God, strives to climb to the top of the wheel. On the left Typhon, the Spirit of Evil, is cast down. The Sphinx, balanced on the top of this wheel, holds a sword in its lion's paws. It personifies Destiny ever ready to strike left or right; according to the direction in which it turns the wheel the humblest rises and the highest is cast down.

Remember, son of Earth, that ability depends on the will; if your will is to be accomplished, you must be daring; and to dare successfully you must be able to keep silence until the moment comes for action. To possess Knowledge and Power, the will must be patient; to remain on the heights of life--if you succeed in attaining them--you must first have learned to plumb with steady gaze vast depths.

ARCANUM XI

[Letter *Caitha* (C, K)--Number 20]

THE TAMED LION: *Strength*

DIVINE WORLD - The Principle of all strength, spiritual or material.

INTELLECTUAL WORLD - Moral Force.

PHYSICAL WORLD - Organic Force.

Arcanum XI is represented by the image of a young girl who with her bare hands is closing, without effort, the jaws of a lion. It is the emblem of that strength which is communicated by faith in oneself and by innocency of life.

Remember, son of Earth, that deeds necessitate faith in your ability to accomplish them. Proceed with faith: all obstacles are phantoms. In order to become strong, silence must be imposed on the weaknesses of the heart; your duty must be studied, for it is the rule of righteousness. Practice justice as if you loved it.

ARCANUM XII

[Letter *Luzain* (L)--Number 30]

THE SACRIFICE: *Violent Death*

DIVINE WORLD - The revelation of the Law.

INTELLECTUAL WORLD - The teaching of Duty.

PHYSICAL WORLD - Sacrifice.

Arcanum XII is represented by a man hung by one foot from a gallows which rests on two trees each of which has six branches cut from the trunk. The hands of this man are tied behind his back, and the bend of his arms forms the base of an inverted triangle the summit of which is his head. It is the sign of violent death encountered by tragic accident or in expiation of some crime, and accepted in a spirit of heroic devotion to Truth and Justice. The twelve lopped branches signify the extinction of life, the destruction of the twelve houses of the Horoscope. The inverted triangle symbolizes catastrophe.

Remember, son of Earth, that devotion is a divine law from which none may have dispensation; but expect nothing, only ingratitude, from men. Let your heart be always ready to tender its account to the Eternal; for if Arcanum XII appears in your horoscope, violent death will lie in wait for you on your path through life. But if the world makes an attempt upon your earthly life, do not die without accepting with resignation the will of God and without pardoning your enemies; for whoever does not forgive shall be condemned, beyond this life, to an eternal solitude.

ARCANUM XIII

[Letter *Mataloth* (M)--Number 40]

THE SCYTHE: *Transformation*

DIVINE WORLD - The perpetual movement of creation, destruction and renewal.

INTELLECTUAL WORLD - The ascent of the Spirit into the divine spheres.

PHYSICAL WORLD - Death, that is, the transformation of human nature on reaching the end of its organic period.

Arcanum XIII is represented by a skeleton scything heads in a meadow; out of the ground on all sides appear men's hands and feet as the scythe pursues its deadly task. It is the emblem of destruction and perpetual rebirth of all forms of Being in the domain of Time.

Remember, son of Earth, that earthly things last only a brief space, and that the highest are cut down like the grass in the fields. The dissolution of your visible organs will come sooner than you expect; but do not fear death, for death is only birth into another life. The universe ceaselessly reabsorbs all that is her own and has not been spiritualized. But the freeing of material instincts by the voluntary adherence of the soul to the laws of universal movement constitutes in us the creation of a second man, the celestial man, and is the beginning of our immortality.

ARCANUM XIV

[Letter *Nain* (N)--Number 50]

THE SOLAR SPIRIT: *Initiative*

DIVINE WORLD - The perpetual movement of life.

INTELLECTUAL WORLD - The combination of the ideas that create morality.

PHYSICAL WORLD - The combination of the forces of Nature.

Arcanum XIV is represented by the Spirit of the Sun holding two urns and pouring from the one into the other the vital sap of life. It is the symbol of the combinations which are ceaselessly produced in all parts of Nature.

Son of Earth, take stock of your strength, not in order to retreat before the works of your hand but in order to wear away obstacles, as water falling drop by drop wears away the hardest stone.

ARCANUM XV

[Letter *Xiron* (X)--Number 60]

TYPHON: *Fate*

DIVINE WORLD - Predestination.

INTELLECTUAL WORLD - Mystery.

PHYSICAL WORLD - The Unforeseen, Fatality.

Arcanum XV is represented by Typhon, the spirit of catastrophes, who rises out of a flaming abyss and brandishes a torch above the heads of two men chained at his feet. It is the image of Fatality which bursts into certain lives like the eruption of a volcano, and overwhelms great as well as small, strong and weak, the cleverest and the least perceptive, in its equal disaster.

Whoever you may be, son of Earth, contemplate the ancient oaks that defy the lightning, but which the lightning strikes after having avoided them for more than a century. Cease to believe in your wisdom and your strength, if God has not granted that you may receive the key to the mysteries that make a prisoner of Fate.

ARCANUM XVI

[Letter *Olelath* (O)--Number 70]

THE LIGHTNING-STRUCK TOWER: *Ruin*

DIVINE WORLD - The punishment of pride.

INTELLECTUAL WORLD - The downfall of the Spirit that attempts to discover the mystery of God.

PHYSICAL WORLD - Reversals of fortune.

Arcanum XVI is represented by a tower struck by lightning. A crowned and an uncrowned man are thrown down from its heights with the ruins of the battlements. It is the symbol of material forces that can crush great and small alike. It is also the emblem of rivalries which only end in ruin for all concerned; of frustrated plans, of hopes that fade away, of abortive enterprises, ruined ambitions and catastrophic deaths.

Remember, son of Earth, that the ordeals of misfortune, accepted with resignation to the supreme Will of the All-Powerful, are the steps in a predestined progress for which you will be eternally rewarded. Suffering is working in order to free yourself from the bonds of material things; it is the putting-on of robes of Immortality.

ARCANUM XVII

[Letter *Pilon* (F, P)--Number 80]

THE STAR OF THE MAGI: *Hope*

DIVINE WORLD - Immortality

INTELLECTUAL WORLD - The Inner Light that illuminates the Spirit.

PHYSICAL WORLD - Hope.

Arcanum XVII is represented by a blazing star with eight rays surrounded by seven other stars hovering over a naked girl who pours over the barren earth the waters of universal Life that flow from two goblets, one gold, the other silver. Beside her, a butterfly is alighting on a rose. This girl is the emblem of Hope which scatters its dew upon our saddest days. She is naked, in order to signify that Hope remains with us when we have been bereft of everything. Above this figure the blazing, eight-pointed star symbolizes the apocalypse of Destinies enclosed by seven seals which are the seven planets, represented by the seven other stars. The butterfly is the sign of resurrection beyond the grave.

Remember, son of Earth, that Hope is the sister of Faith. Abandon your passions and your errors and study the mysteries of true Knowledge, and their key shall be given unto you. Then shall a ray of the divine Light shine from the occult Sanctuary to dispel the darkness of the future and show you the path to happiness. Whatever happens in your life, never break the flowers of Hope, and you will gather the fruits of Faith.

ARCANUM XVIII

[Letter *Tsadi* (TS)--Number 90]

TWILIGHT: *Deceptions*

DIVINE WORLD - The abysses of the Infinite.

INTELLECTUAL WORLD -The darkness that cloaks the Spirit when it submits itself to the power of the instincts.

PHYSICAL WORLD - Deceptions and hidden enemies.

Arcanum XVIII is represented by a field that a half-clouded moon illuminates with a vague twilight. A tower stands on each side of a path that disappears into a barren landscape. In front of one of these two towers a dog is crouching: in front of the other, a dog is baying at the moon: between them is a crab. These towers symbolize the false security which does not foresee hidden perils.

Remember, son of Earth, that whosoever dares to confront the unknown faces death. The hostile spirits, symbolized by one dog, wait in ambush; the servile spirits, symbolized by the other, conceal their treacheries with base flattery; and the idle spirits, symbolized by the crab, will pass by without the slightest concern for disaster. Observe, listen--and learn to keep your own counsel.

ARCANUM XIX

[Letter *Quitolath* (Q)--Number 100]

THE BLAZING LIGHT: *Earthly Happiness*

DIVINE WORLD -The supreme Heaven.

INTELLECTUAL WORLD - Sacred Truth.

PHYSICAL WORLD - Peaceful Happiness.

Arcanum XIX is represented by a radiant sun shining on two small children, images of innocence, who hold each other's hands in the midst of a circle of flowers. It is the symbol of happiness promised by the simple life and by moderation in all one's desires.

Remember, son of Earth, that the light of the Mysteries flows dangerously in the service of the Will. It illuminates those who know how to use it; it strikes down those who are ignorant of its power or who abuse it.

ARCANUM XX

[Letter *Rasith* (R)--Number 200]

THE AWAKENING OF THE DEAD: *Renewal*

Arcanum XX represents the passage from life on earth to the life of the future. A Spirit is blowing a trumpet over a half-open tomb. A man, a woman and a child, a collective symbol of the human trinity, are shown rising from this tomb. It is a sign of the change which is the end of all things, of Good as well as of Evil.

Remember, son of Earth, that fortune is variable, even when it appears most unshakeable. The ascent of the soul is the fruit of its successive ordeals. Hope in the time of suffering, but beware of prosperity. Do not fall asleep in laziness or forgetfulness. At a moment unknown to you the wheel of fortune will turn: you will be raised or cast down by the Sphinx.

ARCANUM O

[Letter *Sichen* (S)--Number 300]

THE CROCODILE: *Expiation*

Arcanum 0 represents the punishment following every error. You can see here a blind man carrying a full beggar's wallet about to collide with a broken obelisk, on which a crocodile is waiting with open jaws. This blind man is the symbol of he who makes himself the slave of material things. His wallet is packed with his errors and his faults. The broken obelisk represents the ruin of his works; the crocodile is the emblem of fate and the inevitable Expiation.

ARCANUM XXI

[Letter *Thoth* (T)--Number 400]

THE CROWN OF THE MAGI: *The Reward*

THIS, the supreme Arcanum of Magism, is represented by a garland of golden roses surrounding a star and placed in a circle around which are set at equal distances the heads of a man, a bull, a lion and an eagle. This is the sign with which the Magus decorates himself when he has reached the highest degree of initiation and has thus acquired a power limited only by his own intelligence and wisdom.